heavenly
chocolate

heavenly
chocolate

RYLAND
PETERS
& SMALL
LONDON NEW YORK

linda collister
photography by **debi treloar**

To my recipe tasters – Emily, Danny and Stevie

Designer	Luis Peral-Aranda
Commissioning Editor	Elsa Petersen-Schepelern
Production	Deborah Wehner
Art Director	Gabriella Le Grazie
Publishing Director	Alison Starling
Food Stylist	Linda Collister
Stylist	Helen Trent
Photographer's Assistant	Lina Ikse Bergman

First published in Great Britain in 2001
by Ryland Peters & Small
Kirkman House
12–14 Whitfield Street
London W1T 2RP
www.rylandpeters.com

10 9 8 7 6 5 4 3 2 1

Text © Linda Collister 2001
Design and photographs © Ryland Peters & Small 2001

ISBN 1 84172 198 0

Printed and bound in China

Author's acknowledgements

I would like to thank the following for their help with this book:
Elsa Petersen-Schepelern, Luis Peral-Aranda, Debi Treloar, Barbara
Levy, Helen Trent, Annette and Will Hertz, Alan and Simon
Silverwood of Alan Silverwood Ltd for loaf tins and baking sheets.
Many thanks also to the Conran Shop, Purves and Purves, and
Kara Kara in London for lending us their beautiful props. And last,
but certainly not least, Alan Hertz.

Notes

All spoon measurements are level unless otherwise stated.
Before baking, weigh or measure all ingredients exactly and prepare
baking tins or sheets.
Make sure your oven has reached the correct temperature before putting in
the recipe to be baked – use an oven thermometer to check the
thermostat is working properly. Every oven is different, so the baking times
can only be guidelines. Recipes in this book were tested in four
different kinds of ovens – all work slightly differently. Consult the
maker's handbook for special instructions.
Some recipes contain raw or lightly cooked eggs. Because of the risk of
transmitting salmonella, these recipes should not be eaten by the elderly,
young children, pregnant women, or those with reduced immune systems.

contents

6   heavenly chocolate ...

10   sweet treats

16   cakes and biscuits

42   chocolate puddings

54   chocolate sauces

58   chocolate drinks

64   index

heavenly chocolate ...

Once, chocolate was thought of as a stimulant and medicine, a cure for hangovers and a source of strength and energy. It was Queen Anne's doctor in the early 18th century who thought of adding milk and feeding it to her sickly children. He eventually sold the recipe to the Quakers, who saw the drink as a healthy alternative to alcohol. Chocolate is now known to contain phosphorous, iron, calcium and theobromine which affects the central nervous system and acts as an anti-depressant, so no wonder it makes us feel good.

These days, chocolate is a rare indulgence for me, as I struggle to eat a balanced diet, but I find the principle of 'a little of what you fancy does you good' actually works: a little top quality chocolate really hits the spot in a way that cheap, sweet, fatty chocolate confectionary bars do not. I get a great kick out of a slice of warm chocolate torte on my birthday, because it is such a special treat, and my taste buds are not jaded.

Using the best ingredients will really make a difference to the taste and quality of any recipe you make. Choose the finest chocolate you can afford, and look out for the organic and fairtrade brands.

Choosing chocolate

The most important rule – read the label before you buy. The best chocolate is made from a blend of beans, rather like coffee, and the flavor depends on the beans used, plus the proportion of cocoa solids and cocoa butter, plus sugar and flavorings. For best taste and final results, choose dark, plain chocolate labelled 'continental style', with cocoa solids around 70 per cent, and pure vanilla essence. Most supermarkets carry own brand, high quality, plain chocolate at fair prices. Plain chocolate with less than 50 per cent cocoa solids will taste very sweet and destroy the flavor of your recipe. It will usually include synthetic flavors and vegetable oils rather than cocoa butter. Avoid very cheap cake covering blocks: they are mostly sugar and vegetable fats. White chocolate does not contain cocoa solids but is made from cocoa butter, sugar and milk solids: avoid children's bars as they will taste greasy and sweet. Milk chocolate contains milk solids instead of some of the cocoa solids, so look out for brands with a high cocoa solid content and pure vanilla.

Storing chocolate

Store chocolate away from other foods in a cool, dry spot. Avoid storing in the fridge or below 13°C, as beads of moisture will form as it returns to room temperature. Working with chocolate is tricky in hot, humid weather or in a steamy kitchen, so try to work when it's cool.

Chopping and grating

In most recipes, chocolate is grated or chopped. In warm weather, chill the chocolate until firm before you start, then use the large-hole side of the grater for grating. Use a clean, dry board and a large knife for chopping. Chocolate can also be chopped in a processor using the pulse button – take care not to overwork the chocolate or it can turn warm and sticky. When chopping chocolate for melting, it's important that the chocolate is cut into evenly sized pieces, so it all melts at the same rate.

Melting chocolate

Chocolate starts to melt at about 30°C (that's why it melts in the mouth), and burns at 110°C. For best results, melt it slowly and gradually, as it easily becomes overheated and scorched and turns into an unusable solid lump. Set the chopped chocolate in a heatproof bowl set over a saucepan of steaming hot but not boiling water. The water must not touch the base of the bowl and don't let a drop of water or steam reach the chocolate or it will seize up. Don't cover the bowl for the same reason. Stir gently and remove the bowl from the heat as soon as the chocolate has melted. If chocolate becomes overheated, and turns into a heavy, rough lump, remove the bowl from the heat and stir in warm vegetable oil, a teaspoon at a time, until smooth again.

Microwaving

Chocolate can also be melted in the microwave, but it should be completely dry inside before you start. It's best to consult the handbook first, but I use the lowest setting and stir and check the progress of the chocolate every minute. It will take less time when melted with butter or a liquid.

sweet treats

christmas prunes

Extra-large pitted prunes, such as Agen or mi-cuit plums, are soaked in brandy or rum then stuffed with marzipan and coated with dark chocolate – try them with coffee after dinner.

Arrange the prunes in a single layer in a shallow dish. Ease them open, then spoon the brandy or rum into the cavity inside each prune so they are well lubricated. Cover and let soak for several hours or overnight.

Divide the marzipan into 12 equal pieces. Using your hands, roll each to a small egg shape, big enough to fill the cavity in the prune. Put a piece of shaped marzipan inside each prune, moulding the prune back into its original form. Set on the lined tray.

Gently melt the chocolate in a heatproof bowl set over a saucepan of steaming but not boiling water. Remove the bowl from the pan and stir gently. Let cool until thickened and almost setting. Using a teaspoon, pour chocolate over each prune to coat – don't worry if they are not perfect as they will look more attractive. Leave in a cool place, but not the refrigerator if possible, until set, then remove from the paper. Store in an airtight container somewhere cool. Best within 5 days.

12 large, pitted, prunes

3 tablespoons brandy or dark rum

115 g best marzipan

100 g plain chocolate, finely chopped

a tray, lined with baking parchment or greaseproof paper

Makes 12

chocolate truffles

Wrap in cellophane and tie with a gorgeous ribbon for an irresistible gift! Truffles are a popular Christmas treat in France and the possibilities for variations are huge – there's even a white truffle.

200 ml double cream

300 g plain chocolate, finely chopped

To coat

250 g plain chocolate, chopped

50 g finest quality cocoa powder, sifted

several trays lined with baking parchment or greaseproof paper

a piping bag with 1.5 cm plain nozzle

Makes 50

Put the cream in a saucepan, gently bring to the boil, then remove from the heat and cool for a minute. Put the chopped chocolate into a heatproof bowl and pour on the hot cream, gently stir a couple of times until smooth, then let cool.

When the mixture is cold but not set, beat vigorously with a wooden spoon until very thick and lighter in colour and texture. Using a teaspoon or piping bag, set marble-sized pieces of the mixture onto the prepared trays. You can also roll the mixture into balls with your hands. Chill until very firm.

When ready to finish the truffles, put the remaining chocolate in a heatproof bowl set over a saucepan of steaming but not boiling water and melt gently. Remove from the heat and stir until smooth. Leave until cool.

Using 2 forks, briefly dip each truffle in the chocolate to coat. Return the coated truffles to the lined trays and leave until the coating chocolate is almost set (if the truffles are very cold this might be immediate), then roll in the cocoa powder. Pack into small boxes and chill. Store in the refrigerator for up to 1 week. Eat at room temperature.

Variations:

Snowball Truffles Coat the chilled truffles in melted white chocolate, then roll in desiccated coconut (optional).

Rum or Brandy Truffles Add 3 tablespoons dark rum or brandy to the chocolate, then add the cream and continue as in the main recipe.

Drambuie or Tia Maria Truffles Add 2 tablespoons Drambuie or Tia Maria as above.

Cherry Liqueur Truffles Add 2 tablespoons syrup from a jar of Morello cherries in Kirsch. Halve cherries if large and drain well on kitchen paper. Push a half into the centre of each shaped truffle and enclose. Let set, then coat and finish.

chocolate and cream fudge

A quick and easy recipe with a rich flavour.

Put the chocolate and butter in a large heatproof bowl set over a saucepan of steaming but not boiling water. Melt gently. Remove the bowl from the pan and gently stir in the cream, then the vanilla or rum, followed by the golden syrup.

Using a wooden spoon, then your hands, work in the icing sugar 1 tablespoon at a time, to make a thick, smooth fudge. If the mixture starts to stiffen before all the sugar has been incorporated, return the bowl to the heat for a minute or so.

Turn the mixture into the prepared tin and press in evenly. Chill in the refrigerator until firm, then turn out and cut into squares with a large sharp knife. Store up to 10 days in the refrigerator.

100 g plain chocolate, finely chopped

55 g unsalted butter

2 tablespoons single or whipping cream

1 teaspoon vanilla essence or dark rum

1 tablespoon golden syrup

225 g icing sugar, sifted

a shallow tin, 18 cm square, buttered

Makes 20 squares

nut fudge

Cut the fudge into squares and store in the refrigerator.

115 g unsalted butter

85 g cocoa powder, sifted

170 g canned evaporated milk

450 g icing sugar, sifted

85 g walnut pieces or toasted hazelnuts

a shallow tin, 18 cm square, buttered

a sugar thermometer

Makes 20 squares

Put the butter in a large, heavy-based saucepan, melt gently, then remove from the heat and stir in the cocoa powder, evaporated milk and, finally, the sugar. Set the pan over low heat and stir constantly until the mixture comes to the boil. Boil gently, stirring frequently to avoid the mixture catching on the bottom of the pan, until the mixture reaches 'soft ball' stage – that is when a sugar thermometer reads 116°C (240°F) or when a little of the fudge dropped from a spoon into a bowl of cold water forms a soft, mouldable ball. This will take about 25 minutes and the mixture will bubble up, so take care.

Remove the pan from the heat, stir in the nuts, pour into the prepared tin and press in evenly with the back of a spoon. Chill until almost set, then mark into squares, cover and chill until firm. Store up to 10 days in the refrigerator.

cakes and biscuits

bûche de noël – yule log

Vanilla sponge

4 large eggs, room temperature

115 g caster sugar

½ teaspoon vanilla essence

135 g plain flour

a good pinch of salt

40 g unsalted butter, melted and cooled

Ganache

175 ml double cream

200 g plain chocolate, finely chopped

Crème pâtissière

200 ml full-cream milk

1 vanilla pod, split lengthways

2 egg yolks

60 g caster sugar

15 g cornflour

To finish

2–3 tablespoons dark rum

icing sugar, for dusting

a baking tray or Swiss roll tin about 25 x 32 cm, greased and lined with baking parchment

greaseproof paper

Makes 1 large cake

Using an electric mixer, electric hand-held whisk or a rotary whisk, beat the eggs, sugar and vanilla vigorously for several minutes until very thick and mousse-like – when you lift the whisk out of the mixture, a thick ribbon-like trail should slowly fall back into the bowl.

Sift the flour and salt over the mixture, then gently fold in with a large, metal spoon. Drizzle the butter over the top and fold it in quickly. Pour the mixture into the prepared tray or tin and spread out to a rectangle about 6 mm thick. Bake in a preheated oven at 220°C (425°F) Gas 7 for about 10 minutes until golden and just firm to the touch. Remove from the oven.

Meanwhile, cover a wire cooling rack with a dry tea towel, then a sheet of baking parchment. Turn out the cooked sponge onto the prepared rack, then peel off the lining paper from the baking tray or tin. Using the tea towel to help you, gently roll up the sponge from the narrow end, along with the parchment, to resemble a Swiss roll. Don't worry if it cracks. Let cool, then wrap in greaseproof paper for up to 24 hours or until ready to assemble.

To make the ganache, heat the cream in a medium saucepan until almost boiling. Remove from the heat, let cool for 1 minute, then tip in the chopped chocolate and stir gently until it has completely melted. Let cool, then beat vigorously until thick. If the mixture begins to separate, add 1 tablespoon chilled cream. Cover and keep at room temperature until ready to assemble, up to 3 hours.

To make the crème pâtissière, pour all but 2 tablespoons of the milk into a medium saucepan. Stir in the vanilla pod and heat gently until the milk is scalding hot but not actually boiling. Cover the pan and leave to infuse for 30 minutes–1 hour. Scrape as many seeds as possible from the pod and stir into the milk, discard the vanilla pod, then reheat the milk. Put the egg yolks, the rest of the milk, sugar and cornflour into a bowl. Stir until smooth. Pour the hot milk onto the mixture, stirring constantly. Pour the whole thing back into

the pan and stir constantly over medium heat until the mixture boils and thickens, about 2–3 minutes. Pour into a clean bowl, press a circle of damp, greaseproof paper onto the surface, let cool, then chill until needed, up to 24 hours.

To assemble, unroll the sponge and peel off and discard the paper. Trim off any hard edges. Sprinkle with the rum, if using. Stir a quarter of the ganache into the crème pâtissière and spread over the sponge, leaving a 3 cm border of sponge all around. Roll up again, as for a Swiss roll, then wrap tightly in foil to maintain the shape. Chill for 1 hour.

Unwrap, set on a cake board or platter and spread the rest of the ganache over the roll to cover completely. Run the back of a fork down the roll to resemble the ridges of the bark, then dip a sharp knife in hot water and cut off each end. Set these ends at one side or on top of the log to resemble sawn-off branches. Dust with icing sugar 'snow' and serve. The assembled log can be covered and kept in a cool place for up to 48 hours.

Nowadays, the French make this cake for Christmas, but its tradition harks back to the pagan Vikings. Their ceremony of the Yule log celebrated the sun at the time of the winter solstice. Yule was Odin, the father of the gods, and a massive log of wood was burned in his honour to bring luck. These days, a small log is burned on Christmas Eve, accompanied by wine and songs, and is always lit by a piece saved from the previous year.

A plain sponge cake with a big difference – cardamom. Widely used in Scandinavia and South India, this attractive pale green spice with its tiny black seeds has a unique and memorable fragrance. This simple cake is also delicious topped with icing.

chocolate, almond and cardamom cake

200 g plain chocolate, finely chopped

4 large eggs, separated

200 g caster sugar

100 g unsalted butter, very soft

100 g ground almonds

the ground black seeds from 4 cardamom pods

70 g self-raising flour

a springform cake tin, 19 cm diameter, greased and base-lined

Makes 1 medium cake

Put the chocolate into a large, heatproof bowl set over a saucepan of steaming but not boiling water. Leave until melted, stirring occasionally. Remove the bowl from the heat and leave until the chocolate feels just warm. Gently stir in the egg yolks, then the sugar. Work in the butter, then the ground almonds, ground cardamom and flour.

Put the egg whites into a clean, dry, grease-free bowl and whisk until stiff. Using a large metal spoon, fold the egg whites into the chocolate mixture in 3 batches.

Spoon into the prepared cake tin and bake in a preheated oven at 180°C (350°F) Gas 4 for about 1 hour or until the mixture springs back when you press it gently with your finger.

Remove from the oven, carefully turn out onto a wire rack and let cool. Wrap in foil, then leave overnight before cutting.

Serve dusted with icing sugar or with whipped cream or ice cream. Best eaten within 5 days.

chocolate cherry cake

Better known as Black Forest Gâteau, I used this recipe as a pastry chef 25 years ago, and the chef who gave it to me has been using it since 1952!

9 large eggs, separated
200 g caster sugar
90 g cocoa powder

Cream and cherry filling

720 g jar Morello cherries in Kirsch syrup or 720 g can or jar Morello cherries in syrup plus 3 tablespoons Kirsch (a 50 ml miniature)
425 ml double or whipping cream
3 tablespoons sugar
55 g plain chocolate, grated

3 sponge sandwich tins, 20.5 cm diameter, greased and base-lined

Makes 1 large cake

Put the egg yolks and sugar into a bowl and whisk until thick and mousse-like – when the whisk is lifted, a wide, ribbon-like trail will slowly fall back into the bowl. Sift the cocoa onto the mixture and gently fold in with a large metal spoon.

Put the egg whites into a spotlessly clean, grease-free bowl and whisk with an electric whisk or mixer, until stiff peaks form. Carefully fold into the yolk mixture in 3 batches. Divide the mixture between the prepared tins, then bake in a preheated oven at 180°C (350°F) Gas 4 for 20–25 minutes until the tops of the cakes spring back when you press them gently with your finger, and have shrunk away from the sides of the tin. Let cool in the tins before unmoulding.

To make the filling, drain the cherries and save the syrup. Leave the cherries on kitchen paper to drain. Reserve 12 to decorate.

Set one of the cooled sponges on a serving plate and sprinkle 2 tablespoons Kirsch syrup over the top.

Put the cream in a bowl and, using an electric whisk or mixer, whip until soft peaks form. Sprinkle the sugar over the cream and whip until slightly thicker. Reserve half the cream to cover the cake. Spread half the remaining cream over the bottom layer of sponge. Press half the cherries into the cream.

Sprinkle the second sponge layer with 2 tablespoons Kirsch syrup as before, then gently set on top of the first layer. Spread with cream and press in the cherries as before. Top with last layer of sponge. Sprinkle with 3 tablespoons Kirsch syrup. Pipe or spread the top and sides of the cake with the reserved cream, then decorate with the reserved cherries and grated chocolate. Chill until ready to serve. Best eaten within 48 hours.

Use the best quality chocolate to produce a good flavour. The sponge can be sprinkled with rum and a little rum can also be added to the dark mousse if you like.

chocolate roulade

6 large eggs, separated

140 g icing sugar, sifted

50 g cocoa powder

1–2 tablespoons rum (optional)

Dark mousse

200 g plain dark chocolate, finely chopped

100 g unsalted butter, diced

4 large eggs, separated

1 tablespoon caster sugar

1–2 tablespoons rum (optional)

White mousse

300 ml double cream, chilled and whipped

100 g best quality white chocolate, grated

To finish

grated dark and white chocolate or sifted icing sugar and cocoa powder

a baking tray, 40 x 35 cm, greased and lined with baking parchment (I use the oven tray that slots into the runners in the oven)

Makes 1 large cake

Put the egg yolks and 100 g of the icing sugar in a bowl and beat until very light and mousse-like – the whisk should leave a ribbon-like trail when lifted out of the bowl. Sift the cocoa into the bowl and gently fold in with a large metal spoon. Put the egg whites in a bowl and whisk until soft peaks form. Whisk in the remaining icing sugar, 1 tablespoon at a time, until stiff peaks form. Fold into the yolk mixture in 3 batches. Gently spread an even layer of mixture on the prepared tray, then bake in a preheated oven at 190°C (375°F) Gas 5 for 8–10 minutes until firm to the touch.

Meanwhile, cover a wire cooling rack with a damp tea towel topped with a sheet of baking parchment. Tip the cooked sponge onto the rack, then lift off the baking tray, peel the parchment off the bottom and let cool.

To make the dark mousse, put the chocolate and butter in a heatproof bowl set over a saucepan of steaming not boiling water and melt gently. Remove from the heat and gently stir in the yolks, then the rum, if using. Let cool. Put the egg whites in a bowl, whisk until stiff, then add the sugar and whisk again until stiff. Fold into the chocolate mixture in 3 batches. Chill briefly until starting to set.

To make the white mousse, chill the whipped cream if necessary, then fold in the grated chocolate and chill until ready to assemble.

To assemble, sprinkle the sponge with rum, if using. Spread the dark mousse mixture on top, leaving a 2 cm border of sponge all around. Cover with white mousse, then roll up from the narrow end like a Swiss roll, using the baking parchment to help you. Wrap in the parchment to give it a neat shape then chill for 30 minutes–2 hours.

When ready to serve, remove the paper and transfer the roll to a serving plate. Decorate with grated chocolate or icing sugar and cocoa.

Adding a touch of cocoa to the usual biscuit crust gives an extra boost to this easy recipe.

chocolate chip cheesecake

Biscuit crust

150 g digestive biscuits, crushed

1 tablespoon cocoa powder

40 g golden caster sugar

70 g unsalted butter, melted

Chocolate filling

500 g cream cheese

1 teaspoon vanilla essence

125 g caster sugar

3 large eggs, lightly beaten

250 ml sour cream

100 g plain chocolate, finely chopped, or choc chips

cocoa powder, for dusting

a springform cake tin, 22 cm diameter, well greased

a baking sheet

Serves 8

To make the crust, put the biscuit crumbs in a bowl, mix in the cocoa powder and sugar, then stir in the melted butter. Tip into the prepared tin and press firmly onto the base and halfway up the sides with the back of a spoon. Chill while making the filling.

Put the cream cheese, vanilla and sugar into the bowl of an electric mixer and mix at low speed until very smooth. (You can also use a wooden spoon, but it's hard work.) Gradually beat in the eggs, increasing the speed as the mixture softens. Finally, beat in the sour cream. Using a large metal spoon, stir in the chopped chocolate.

Pour the filling into the crust, set the tin on the baking sheet and bake in a preheated oven at 150°C (300°F) Gas 2 for about 1¼ hours or until just firm. The cheesecake will probably sink as it cools, then crack, so turn off the oven and leave the door slightly ajar. Leave the cheesecake to cool slowly in the falling temperature for about 1 hour. Remove from the oven and let cool completely on a wire rack. Cover and chill overnight before unclipping the tin. Serve dusted with cocoa. Best eaten within 4 days – store well covered in the refrigerator.

175 ml full-cream milk

60 g plain chocolate, finely chopped

125 g caster sugar

60 g unsalted butter, at room temperature

½ teaspoon vanilla essence

1 large egg, beaten

150 g self-raising flour

Fudge topping

100 g plain chocolate, finely chopped

1 tablespoon golden syrup

25 g unsalted butter, at room temperature

12-hole deep muffin or bun tin, lined with paper cake cases

Makes 12

Put the milk in a saucepan and heat until scalding hot but not boiling. Put the chocolate into a bowl, add about one-third of the sugar, then pour over the hot milk and stir until smooth and melted. Let cool.

Put the butter in a bowl, add the vanilla and remaining sugar. Using an electric mixer or wooden spoon, beat until light and fluffy, then gradually beat in the egg. Working in batches, stir in the chocolate mixture alternately with the flour. Mix well to make a smooth, thick batter. Pour or spoon into the paper cake cases until half full.

Bake in a preheated oven at 180°C (350°F) Gas 4 for 15–18 minutes or until well risen, and the cakes spring back when gently pressed with your finger. Remove from the oven and let cool on a wire rack.

To make the fudge topping, which can be used for large sponge cakes as well as small cupcakes and fairy cakes, put the chocolate in the top of a double boiler, or in a heatproof bowl set over a saucepan of steaming but not boiling water, and melt gently. Remove the bowl from the pan and stir in the syrup and butter. When smooth, let cool, stirring occasionally. When very thick and on the point of setting, dip the top of each little cake into the fudge topping (or spread it on) until thickly coated. Let set until firm. Best eaten within 3 days.

old fashioned cupcakes

These individual cakes, with a light moist crumb and fudgy topping, were the after-school treat for generations of deserving children. The first is that they were baked in cups. The second is that it came from the original recipe measurements; four cups flour, three cups sugar, and one of melted butter – this recipe is slightly smaller!

choc chip banana muffins

2 ripe, medium bananas

115 g unsalted butter, at room temperature

85 g light muscovado sugar

1 large egg, beaten

50 g walnut pieces

50 g plain chocolate, coarsely chopped, or choc chips

225 g self-raising flour

12-hole deep muffin tin,
well greased or lined with paper
muffin cases

Makes 12

Mash the bananas with a fork (they should not be too smooth) and set aside.

Put the butter in a bowl and, using an electric mixer or wooden spoon, beat until creamy, then beat in the sugar. When the mixture is light and fluffy, gradually beat in the egg.

Using a large metal spoon, stir in the bananas, nuts and chocolate or choc chips. Add the flour and gently fold in to make a coarse-looking mixture: to avoid a tough end result, try to use as few movements as possible. Spoon into the prepared muffin tin and bake immediately in a preheated oven at 200°C (400°F) Gas 6 for 15–20 minutes until golden brown, well risen, and firm to the touch. Let cool for a minute then gently unmould, using a round-bladed knife to loosen the muffins. Cool on a wire rack and eat while still warm, or the same day.

choc chip muffins

Sift the flour with the cocoa, baking powder, bicarbonate of soda and salt into a bowl. Set aside.

Put the butter in a bowl and, using an electric mixer or wooden spoon, beat until creamy, then gradually beat in the eggs and vanilla essence. When the mixture is light and fluffy, stir in the sour cream, then 100 g of the chocolate until well mixed. Add the flour mixture and stir briefly until barely mixed.

Spoon into the prepared muffin tin, sprinkle with the chopped chocolate topping and bake in the preheated oven at 200°C (400°F) Gas 6 for 20–25 minutes until firm to the touch. Let cool for a minute then carefully unmould and cool on a wire rack. Eat while still warm or the same day.

250 g plain flour

40 g cocoa powder

1 teaspoon baking powder

1 teaspoon bicarbonate of soda

a pinch of salt

115 g unsalted butter, at room temperature

100 g caster sugar

½ teaspoon vanilla essence

2 large eggs, lightly beaten

230 ml sour cream

150 g plain chocolate, coarsely chopped, or choc chips

12-hole deep muffin tin, well greased or lined with paper muffin cases

Makes 12

Eaten warm for breakfast all over America, muffins should have a coarser crumb than fairy cakes or cupcakes and a more robust, less sweet taste.

Two shortbread doughs – one vanilla, one chocolate – are rolled together, then sliced into spectacular biscuits. For the best taste, only butter will do – and the traditional ground rice adds the authentic grainy texture.

pinwheel biscuits

Put the butter in a bowl and, using an electric mixer or a wooden spoon, beat until creamy, then gradually beat in the sugar. Continue beating until the mixture becomes light and fluffy, then beat in the vanilla.

Put half of the mixture into another bowl. Sift the ground rice, rice flour or cornflour and half the flour onto one mixture, then sift the remaining flour and the cocoa onto the other mixture. Work each mixture using a wooden spoon or your hands to make a stiff dough. In hot weather, wrap each piece of dough in greaseproof paper and chill until firm.

Set the plain dough in the middle of a sheet of greaseproof paper and, using a well-floured rolling pin, roll out to a rectangle about 22 x 28 cm. Roll out the chocolate dough on a second sheet of paper in the same way. Gently invert the chocolate dough on top of the plain dough, neaten the edges with your hands, then very carefully roll it up, starting from one long side, rather like a Swiss roll. Don't worry if any cracks appear – just press them together with your fingers. Wrap the long, slim roll in greaseproof paper and chill for 15 minutes or until very firm.

300 g unsalted butter, at room temperature

150 g golden caster sugar

½ teaspoon vanilla essence

400 g plain flour

25 g ground rice, rice flour or cornflour

25 g cocoa powder, sifted

several baking sheets, greased

Makes 28

Using a long, sharp knife, cut the roll into 1 cm thick slices. Arrange slightly apart on the prepared baking sheets, then bake in a preheated oven at 180°C (350°F) Gas 4 for 12–15 minutes until firm and slightly golden at the edges. Cool for a couple of minutes until firm, then transfer to a wire rack to cool. When completely cold, store in an airtight container. Eat within 1 week or freeze for up to 1 month.

These cookies were first made (without chocolate) in medieval German monasteries. The most famous come from Nüremburg, a centre of the spice trade in the 16th century, when chocolate first arrived in Europe. One snowy December, I visited a small bakery working around the clock to make enough for the Advent Market. The baker told me that the recipe differs from other German ones in that it is based on meringue, as many as seven spices, and nuts rather than honey and flour.

lebkuchen

100 g unblanched almonds (with brown skins left on)

25 g plain chocolate, coarsely chopped

2 tablespoons very finely chopped mixed peel

½ teaspoon ground cinnamon

½ teaspoon ground ginger

¼ teaspoon grated nutmeg

¼ teaspoon ground black pepper

¼ teaspoon ground cloves

¼ teaspoon ground allspice

2 large egg whites

115 g icing sugar, sifted

Chocolate glaze

100 g plain chocolate, finely chopped

100 g icing sugar, sifted

several baking sheets, lined with baking parchment

Makes 12

Put the almonds and chocolate into a food processor and work until finely ground. Thoroughly mix with the mixed peel and spices.

Put the egg whites in a spotlessly clean bowl and, using an electric whisk or mixer, whisk until stiff peaks form. Gradually whisk in the icing sugar, then whisk for a further minute or so to make a very thick, glossy meringue. Add the ground almond and chocolate mixture and carefully fold in with a large metal spoon.

Put tablespoon-sized mounds of the mixture on the prepared baking sheets, setting them well apart, then spread each into a neat circle about 9 cm in diameter. If you're feeling creative you can make heart shapes with the mixture.

Bake in a preheated oven at 160°C (325°F) Gas 3 for 15–20 minutes until the cookies are pale gold. Let cool, then peel off the parchment.

Meanwhile, to make the chocolate glaze, put the chocolate in a bowl, set it over a saucepan of steaming water and melt gently. Remove and cool. Mix the sifted icing sugar with 4 tablespoons hot water to make a smooth glacé icing, then stir in the chocolate to make a fairly runny mixture – if necessary, stir in a little extra warm water. Dip each cookie in the glaze to coat thinly, then leave to set on waxed paper. Store in an airtight container. Eat within 1 week.

speckled cookies

Using an electric mixer, whisk or wooden spoon, beat the butter until creamy. Add the icing sugar and beat, slowly at first, until light and fluffy. Beat in the vanilla essence, then stir in the oats.

Sift the flour, salt and baking powder into the bowl and mix with a wooden spoon or your hands to make a stiff dough.

Shape the dough into a log about 7 cm in diameter, then wrap in greaseproof paper and chill for 20 minutes until firm.

Slice the log into rounds about 6 mm thick. Grate the chocolate and sprinkle about 1 teaspoon on the top of each round. Set the rounds slightly apart on the prepared sheet. Bake in a preheated oven at 160°C (325°F) Gas 3 for 20 minutes until lightly golden around the edges. Leave the cookies on the sheet for a couple of minutes to firm up, then transfer to a wire cooling rack to cool completely. Store in an airtight container. Eat within 5 days or freeze for up to 1 month.

200 g unsalted butter, at room temperature

100 g icing sugar, sifted

1 teaspoon vanilla essence

75 g porridge oats

225 g plain flour

a pinch of salt

½ teaspoon baking powder

40 g plain chocolate, chilled

several baking sheets, greased

Makes 20

Wonderfully easy, attractive cookies that manage the impossible: they crumble in the hand, then melt in the mouth.

choc chip maple pecan biscuits

Put the butter in a bowl and, using an electric mixer or wooden spoon, beat until creamy. Beat in the sugar and maple syrup until light and fluffy. Gradually beat in the egg then, using your hands or a wooden spoon, work in the flour, chocolate and nuts to make a rather soft dough. Using well-floured hands, shape the dough into a log 23 x 5 cm thick. Wrap in greaseproof paper and chill overnight or for 2 hours in the freezer (the uncooked dough can be stored in the refrigerator for up to 5 days or up to 1 month in the freezer).

Unwrap the dough, cut into 5 mm slices, then arrange well apart on the prepared trays. Bake in a preheated oven at 200°C (400°F) Gas 6 for 10–12 minutes until pale gold. Leave on the sheets for a few minutes to firm up then transfer to wire racks to cool. Store in an airtight container and eat within 1 week or freeze for up to 1 month.

175 g unsalted butter, at room temperature

140 g light muscovado sugar

2 tablespoons maple syrup

1 medium egg, lightly beaten

300 g self-raising flour

50 g plain chocolate, coarsely chopped, or choc chips

50 g pecan nuts, chopped

several baking sheets, well greased

Makes 36

chocolate pecan chunkies

200 g plain chocolate, chopped

55 g unsalted butter, at room temperature

2 large eggs, at room temperature

140 g golden caster sugar

½ teaspoon vanilla essence

3 tablespoons self-raising flour

100 g plain or white chocolate, chopped, or choc chips

100 g pecan or walnut pieces

several baking sheets, greased and lined

Makes 22

Put the chocolate in a heatproof bowl set over a saucepan of steaming but not boiling water and melt gently. Remove the bowl, stir in the butter and let cool.

Put the eggs, sugar and vanilla in a large bowl and, using an electric mixer or rotary whisk, beat until very thick and mousse-like. When you lift the whisk, a thick, ribbon-like trail should fall back into the bowl.

Sift the flour into the mixture and carefully fold in with a large metal spoon. Gently fold in the chocolate mixture, then the chopped chocolate or choc chips and nuts. Put tablespoon-sized mounds of the mixture onto the prepared baking sheets, setting well apart, because the mixture spreads. Bake in a preheated oven at 180°C (350°F) Gas 4 for about 10 minutes until barely set. Let cool and firm up on the trays, then transfer to wire cooling racks. Store an airtight container and eat within 1 week or freeze for up to 1 month.

soft and fudgy brownies

This is my mother-in-law's recipe for very soft and fudgy brownies. The original recipe comes from a dog-eared newspaper clipping, circa 1950, of Church bakes. Over the years, the sugar has been reduced and the nuts omitted altogether to please her grandchildren, but she insists on slight undercooking to get the right, gooey texture.

115 g unsalted butter, at room temperature

300 g caster sugar

5 large eggs, lightly beaten

1 teaspoon vanilla essence

70 g plain flour

70 g cocoa powder

230 g plain chocolate, melted and cooled

a cake tin, about 22.5 x 27.5 cm, greased and base-lined

Makes 30

Put the butter and sugar in a bowl and beat until soft and fluffy, then beat in the vanilla. Gradually beat in the eggs, a little at a time. Sift the flour with cocoa into the bowl and stir well. Lastly, mix in the melted chocolate. Spoon into the prepared tin and spread evenly.

Bake in a preheated oven at 160°C (325°F) Gas 3 for about 20 minutes until almost firm to the touch. Let cool, then cut into tiny squares and remove from the tin. Store in lidded container and eat within 3 days.

Best eaten warm with vanilla ice cream.

chocolate
puddings

choc chunk crunch ice cream

Mix the breadcrumbs with the muscovado sugar and spread over the base of the baking tin. Bake in a preheated oven at 200°F (400°C) Gas 6, stirring frequently, for about 10–15 minutes until the mixture is a dark golden brown. Let cool completely, then break up the lumps and mix with the chopped chocolate.

Put the cream in a bowl and, using an electric mixer or whisk, whip until it stands in soft peaks. Whisk in the vanilla and sugar. Spoon into an ice cream maker and freeze until slushy and almost frozen. Alternatively, spoon into a freezer-proof container, then freeze and stir every 10 minutes or so until slushy.

Stir in the chocolate mixture and freeze again until firm. If not using immediately, transfer the ice cream to a suitable lidded container and store in the freezer for up to 1 week. Serve with one of the hot chocolate sauces (page 56–7).

85 g wholemeal breadcrumbs

85 g light muscovado sugar

85 g plain chocolate, finely chopped

300 ml double cream, well chilled

1 teaspoon vanilla essence

1½ tablespoons caster sugar

a baking tin, lightly oiled

Serves 4–6

choc spice ice

200 g plain chocolate, finely chopped

275 ml milk

1 cinnamon stick or ½ teaspoon ground cinnamon

3 large egg yolks

75 g caster sugar

200 ml double or whipping cream, well chilled

Serves 4–6

Put the chopped chocolate into a large, heatproof bowl.

Put the milk and the cinnamon stick or ground cinnamon in a saucepan, heat until almost boiling, then cover the pan and leave to infuse for 15 minutes.

Put the egg yolks and sugar in a heatproof bowl and stir well. Gently reheat the milk, remove the cinnamon stick, then pour the hot milk onto the egg mixture, stirring constantly. When well mixed, pour the mixture back into the saucepan. Stir gently over low heat until the mixture thickens into a custard – don't let it boil or it will curdle. Remove from the heat, then pour the custard over the chopped chocolate and stir gently until smooth. Let cool, then cover and chill.

Whip the cream until it forms soft peaks, then fold in the cold chocolate mixture. Pour into an ice cream maker and churn until frozen. Eat immediately or store in the freezer. Alternatively, freeze in a freezer-proof container, stirring occasionally.

easy chocolate mousse

This classic French recipe has been going strong for many generations; my mother learned to make it when she lived in Paris in the 1930s. It can easily be halved or doubled and served in a large bowl or individual cups, glasses or dishes, with crisp biscuits.

Put the chocolate and water, coffee, brandy or rum into a heatproof bowl set over a saucepan of steaming but not boiling water and melt very gently, taking care not to overheat the chocolate.

Remove from the heat and gently stir in the butter. Let cool for 1 minute, then gently stir in the yolks, one at a time.

Put the whites into a spotlessly clean, grease-free bowl and whisk until stiff peaks form, using an electric mixer or a balloon whisk. Mix about 1 tablespoon into the chocolate mixture to soften it. Fold in the rest of the whites in 3 batches using a large metal spoon until just combined – do not overmix.

Carefully spoon into a serving bowl or individual dishes; you can serve coffee-flavoured chocolate mousse in tiny cups set on saucers or – for mousse made with alcohol – use brandy or champagne or pretty crystal glasses. This mousse is very rich. Chill for at least 2 hours before serving. Best eaten within 12 hours.

125 g plain chocolate, finely chopped

2 tablespoons water, strong black coffee, brandy or rum

15 g unsalted butter, at room temperature

4 large eggs, separated

a glass bowl, coffee cups, brandy glasses, champagne flutes or sundae dishes

Serves 4–6

If you've never tried your hand at a steamed pudding, try this one – comfort food at its very best. The mixture is classic chocolate sponge but with ground almonds for a richer flavour. Steaming makes the texture light-as-a-feather, a once-eaten never-forgotten treat. Serve with a sauce from pages 56–57 (I think the custard is best).

115 g unsalted butter, at room temperature

115 g caster sugar

2 large eggs, lightly beaten

85 g self-raising flour

½ teaspoon baking powder

30 g ground almonds

2 tablespoons cocoa powder

1 tablespoon milk

chocolate custard (page 57), to serve

a heatproof pudding basin, about 900 ml, well buttered

a large sheet of foil

Serves 6

Pour water into a large saucepan until about one-third full. Put an old saucer upside-down in the pan, then bring to the boil, ready to cook the pudding. You can also use a steamer.

Put the butter in a bowl and, using an electric mixer or a wooden spoon, beat until creamy. Add the sugar and beat until the mixture is very light and fluffy. Gradually beat in the eggs, beating well after each addition. Sift the flour with the baking powder, almonds and cocoa then, using a large metal spoon, fold it into the beaten mixture with the milk. Spoon the mixture into the prepared basin, about two-thirds full. Cut a large square of foil, and butter one side. Fold the foil down the middle to make a large pleat (to let the pudding expand), then put the foil over the top of the bowl, buttered side down.

Tie the foil tightly around the top of the bowl with string (make a string handle too if possible), then set the bowl onto the saucer in the saucepan – the water level should come halfway up the sides of the bowl, so pour out any excess water or top up with extra boiling water. Cover the pan and boil the pudding steadily for about 1½ hours until firm, topping up the water from time to time to prevent the pan boiling dry.

Remove from the saucepan and carefully remove the foil. Loosen the pudding with a round-bladed knife, turn out onto a warmed plate and serve with custard.

steamed chocolate pudding
with hot chocolate custard

upside-down pear pudding

100 g plain chocolate, finely chopped

100 g unsalted butter, at room temperature

100 g light muscovado sugar, sifted

2 large eggs, beaten

3 pieces stem ginger, finely chopped, plus 3 tablespoons syrup from the jar

125 g self-raising flour

Pear topping

40 g unsalted butter

40 g light muscovado sugar

2 large or 3 small pears, peeled, cored and quartered

a tarte Tatin tin or cake tin (not springform), 22 cm diameter, greased

Serves 8

To make the pear topping, put the butter in a small saucepan, heat until melted, then stir in the sugar. When smooth and the sugar has dissolved, pour the mixture into the base of the pan. Arrange the pears, rounded side down, on top of the mixture.

Put the chocolate in a heatproof bowl set over a saucepan of steaming but not boiling water. Melt very gently. Remove and let cool while making the batter.

Put the butter in a bowl and, using an electric mixer or wooden spoon, beat until creamy. Beat in the sugar. Continue beating until fluffy, then gradually beat in the eggs, followed by the chopped ginger, ginger syrup and the melted chocolate. Fold in the flour with a large metal spoon and, when well mixed, spread the batter on top of the fruit in the tin and level the surface.

Bake in a preheated oven at 180°C (350°F) Gas 4 for 45–60 minutes until firm to the touch, then turn out onto a warmed serving plate to reveal the sticky pear topping. Serve warm with ice cream or whipped cream, a chocolate sauce or chocolate custard (pages 56–57). It can also be left to cool and eaten as a cake.

A good pudding for a winter Sunday lunch – pears and chocolate make one of the happiest combinations.

Pavlova

3 egg whites

a pinch of salt

175 g light muscovado sugar, sifted

1 teaspoon cornflour

½ teaspoon vanilla essence

1 teaspoon white wine vinegar

Chocolate-chestnut topping

300 ml double or whipping cream, well chilled

2 tablespoons caster sugar

2 tablespoons dark rum (optional)

100 g plain chocolate, grated

400 g canned chestnuts in syrup, drained weight 200 g

a baking sheet lined with baking parchment

Serves 6

To make the pavlova, put the egg whites and salt into a spotlessly clean, grease-free bowl and whisk with an electric mixer or whisk, until they form stiff peaks. Gradually whisk in half of the sugar, the cornflour and vanilla to make a stiff meringue. Using a large metal spoon, gently fold in the rest of the sugar – don't overwork, or the mixture will turn sticky.

Spoon the mixture onto the prepared baking sheet to make a circle about 23 cm diameter and 3 cm deep. Make a shallow dip in the middle.

Bake in a preheated oven at 150°C (300°F) Gas 2 for 1–1¼ hours until very crisp on the outside and slightly soft in the middle. Turn off the oven and leave the pavlova to cool inside. Remove from the oven, peel away the baking parchment and set the pavlova on a large serving plate. Don't worry if any cracks form.

To make the topping, put the cream in a large bowl and whisk with an electric mixer or whisk, until it stands in soft peaks. Whisk in the sugar and rum, if using, and whisk until almost stiff. Carefully fold in half of the chocolate and all the chestnuts.

Pile the mixture on top of the pavlova, then sprinkle with the remaining chocolate. Serve immediately or chill and serve the same day with chocolate sauce.

chocolate pavlova
with chocolate and chestnuts

A combination of crunchy and sticky meringue plus whipped cream, grated chocolate and sweet chestnuts makes a special holiday-time pudding. Serve with the Rich Dark Chocolate Sauce on page 56.

warm chocolate torte

Not a pudding, or a cake, or even a mousse, this flourless concoction defies categorization – but is easy to achieve. Eat it warm with plenty of vanilla ice cream and beautiful fresh berries, such as raspberries or blueberries.

Put the chocolate in a heatproof bowl set over a saucepan of steaming but not boiling water and let it melt gently. Remove the bowl from the pan, stir the chocolate gently until smooth, then set aside. Alternatively, use a double-boiler.

Put the butter into a bowl and, using an electric mixer, balloon whisk or wooden spoon, beat until creamy. Add the sugar and beat until light and fluffy. Beat in the egg yolks, one at a time, and beating well after each addition. Beat in the cooled chocolate and the vanilla or coffee. Using a large metal spoon, stir in the ground almonds.

Put the egg whites and salt in a spotlessly clean, grease-free bowl and, using a balloon whisk or an electric mixer, whisk until they form soft peaks.

Using a large metal spoon, gently fold the egg whites into the chocolate mixture in 3 batches. Spoon the mixture into the prepared cake tin and bake in a preheated oven at 200°C (400°F) Gas 6 for 10 minutes. Then reduce the oven temperature to 180°C (350°F) Gas 4 and bake for a further 7–10 minutes until barely set – do not overcook or the torte will be dry.

Remove from the oven and set the tin on a wet tea towel. Do not unmould the cake, but run a round-bladed knife around the side of the tin to loosen the cake. Leave for 10–15 minutes, then gently unmould, dust with icing sugar and serve warm, with whipped cream and raspberries or with vanilla ice cream. Alternatively, leave until completely cold, then unmould and wrap in foil. Store at room temperature for up to 48 hours, then gently warm before serving.

125 g plain chocolate, finely chopped

115 g unsalted butter, at room temperature

85 g caster sugar

4 large eggs, separated

½ teaspoon vanilla essence or 1 tablespoon extra strong (espresso) coffee

115 g ground almonds

a pinch of salt

icing sugar, for dusting

a springform cake tin, 20.5 cm diameter, greased and base-lined

Serves 6–8

chocolate sauces

rich dark chocolate sauce

To make a creamy variation of this sauce, use single cream instead of the water or, for a flavoured sauce, use a tablespoon or so of brandy, rum or coffee liqueur instead of some of the water.

100 g plain dark chocolate, finely chopped
60 g unsalted butter, diced

Serves 4–6

Put the chopped chocolate, butter and 100 ml water in a heatproof bowl set over a saucepan of steaming not boiling water. Stir frequently until melted and very smooth. Remove from the heat and stir well until glossy and slightly thickened. As the sauce cools it will become even thicker. Serve warm.

creamy chocolate sauce

A very quick, rich sauce for ice cream, profiteroles and steamed puddings. Just before serving, it can be flavoured with rum, brandy or coffee liqueur to taste. For a slightly thinner and less rich sauce use single cream, or cream mixed half and half with milk or coffee.

Put the cream into a small, heavy-based saucepan and heat gently, stirring frequently. When the cream comes to the boil, remove the pan from the heat, let cool for a minute, then stir in the chopped chocolate. Stir gently until the sauce is smooth. Stir in the vanilla and serve immediately.

125 ml double cream
85 g plain dark chocolate, finely chopped
½ teaspoon vanilla essence

Serves 4–6

chocolate custard

The classic sauce for steamed puddings.

450 ml creamy milk

3 tablespoons cocoa powder

60 g caster sugar

1 tablespoon cornflour

2 egg yolks

Serves 4–6

Put all but 2 tablespoons of the milk in a large saucepan and heat until almost boiling. Sift the cocoa, sugar and cornflour into a heatproof bowl, stir in the egg yolks and milk to make a thick paste, then stir in the hot milk. Strain the mixture back into the saucepan and stir constantly over low heat until the mixture thickens – don't let the mixture boil or it will separate.

Remove the custard from the heat and use at once, or keep it warm until ready to serve.

white chocolate sauce

The flavour depends on the quality of the chocolate, so use the best you can lay your hands on rather than children's bars.

Put the chocolate in a heatproof bowl set over a saucepan of steaming but not boiling water and melt gently. Remove the bowl from the heat and stir gently until smooth.

Put the cream and milk in a saucepan and heat until scalding hot, but not quite boiling. Remove from the heat. Pour onto the chocolate in a thin stream, whisking the mixture constantly, to make a smooth sauce. Pour into a warmed jug and serve at once with puddings or ice cream, or let cool and serve with red berries or Warm Chocolate Torte (page 52).

200 g good quality white chocolate, finely chopped

200 ml double cream

80 ml creamy milk

Serves 4–6

chocolate drinks

Don't wait for snow! Have this hot chocolate any time.

the best hot chocolate

85 g plain chocolate, broken into pieces

1 tablespoon caster sugar, or to taste

1 vanilla pod, split lengthways

300 ml creamy milk

100 ml whipping cream, whipped

grated chocolate or cocoa powder, for sprinkling

Serves 2

Put the chocolate pieces, sugar, vanilla and milk into a small, heavy-based saucepan. Heat gently, stirring, until the chocolate has melted, then bring to the boil, whisking constantly until very smooth and frothy. Remove the vanilla pod. Pour into warmed mugs, top with whipped cream and a sprinkling of chocolate or cocoa, then serve.

100 g plain chocolate, broken into pieces

450 ml creamy milk

2 tablespoons vodka

100 ml whipping cream, whipped (optional)

grated chocolate or cocoa, for sprinkling

Serves 2

Put the chocolate and half the milk into a small, heavy-based saucepan and heat gently, stirring constantly, until melted. Add the rest of the milk and heat, stirring frequently, until piping hot and smoothly blended. Pour into warmed mugs, add the vodka, then top with the whipped cream, if using, and the grated chocolate or cocoa. Drink very hot.

Not one to share with the kids.

hot russian

hot spanish

Dip long cinnamon sticks in melted chocolate, let set, then use as stirring spoons for this traditional drink.

50 g plain chocolate, broken into pieces

225 ml creamy milk

1 tablespoon caster sugar

1 cinnamon stick

300 ml hot, strong black coffee

2 tablespoons brandy (optional)

4 curls fresh orange peel

Serves 4

Put the chocolate, milk, sugar and cinnamon stick in a saucepan and heat gently, stirring constantly, until smooth and melted. Bring to the boil, whisking, then remove from the heat and whisk in the coffee and brandy, if using. Remove the cinnamon stick. Put the orange peel into tall, warmed, heatproof glasses and pour over the hot mixture.

100 g plain chocolate, broken into pieces

1 tablespoon caster sugar, or to taste

300 ml creamy milk

450 ml freshly made, hot, strong black coffee

100 ml whipping cream, whipped

Serves 4

Put the chocolate, sugar and milk into a heavy-based saucepan and stir over a low heat until melted and smooth. Bring to the boil, whisking constantly ,then remove from the heat and whisk in the fresh, hot coffee. Pour into warmed mugs and top with whipped cream.

The classic chocolate-coffee combo.

hot mocha

iced mocha

A chilled-down version of Hot Mocha (page 61) using ice cream and ice cubes instead of whipped cream.

100 g plain chocolate, broken into pieces

1 tablespoon caster sugar, or to taste

300 ml creamy milk

450 ml hot, strong black coffee

85 g vanilla ice cream (optional)

ice cubes, to serve

Serves 4

Put the chocolate, sugar and milk into a heavy-based saucepan and stir over low heat until melted and smooth. Bring to the boil, whisking constantly. Remove from the heat and whisk in the freshly made hot coffee. Let cool, then chill. Put in a blender, add the ice cream, if using, then blend until smooth. Fill tall, chilled glasses with ice cubes, then pour over the mocha drink and serve.

chocolate milkshake

Chocolate is everyone's favourite milkshake.
The ice cubes will make it lightly frothy.

Put the milk, drinking chocolate and ice cubes into a blender and pulse briefly until smooth. Put a scoop of ice cream into each of 4 chilled tall glasses. Pour over the milkshake, sprinkle with a little grated chocolate or sprinkles and serve with straws.

700 ml creamy milk, well chilled

6 tablespoons drinking chocolate powder

6 ice cubes

4 scoops chocolate ice cream, about 100 g

grated chocolate or chocolate sprinkles, to serve

Serves 4

index

biscuits:

    choc chip maple pecan, 38

    chocolate pecan chunkies, 38

    lebkuchen, 34

    pinwheel, 33

    soft and fudgy brownies, 41

    speckled cookies, 36

büche de noël – yule log, 18

cakes:

    chocolate, almond and cardamom cake, 21

    chocolate cherry cake, 22

    chocolate chip cheesecake, 26

    chocolate roulade, 25

    old fashioned cupcakes, 29

cakes and biscuits, 16–41

chocolate drinks, 58–63

    best hot chocolate, 60

    chocolate milkshake, 63

    iced mocha, 63

    hot mocha, 61

    hot Russian, 60

    hot Spanish, 61

chocolate puddings, 42–53

chocolate sauces, 54–57

    chocolate custard, 57

    creamy chocolate sauce, 56

    rich dark chocolate sauce, 56

    white chocolate sauce, 57

choosing chocolate, 8

chopping chocolate, 8

Christmas prunes, 12

cupcakes, old fashioned, 29

easy chocolate mousse, 45

fudge:

    chocolate and cream, 15

    nut, 15

hot chocolate pudding, 46

ice cream:

    choc chunk crunch ice cream, 44

    choc spice ice, 44

melting chocolate, 8

microwaving chocolate, 8

mousse, easy chocolate, 45

muffins:

    choc chip banana, 30

    choc chip, 30

nut fudge, 15

pavlova, chocolate, with chocolate and chestnuts, 51

pear, upside-down pear pudding, 49

pinwheel biscuits, 33

prunes, Christmas, 12

pudding:

    hot chocolate, 46

    upside-down pear pudding, 49

storing chocolate, 8

sweet treats, 10–15

torte, warm chocolate, 52

truffles:

    cherry liqueur, 13

    chocolate, 13

    Drambuie or Tia Maria, 13

    rum or brandy, 13

    snowball, 13

upside down pear pudding, 48

warm chocolate torte, 52

white chocolate:

    sauce, 57

    snowball truffles, 13

yule log, 18